As IRON *Sharpens* IRON

RYAN BROWN

ISBN 979-8-88685-003-1 (paperback)
ISBN 979-8-88685-004-8 (digital)

Christian Faith Publishing
832 Park Avenue
Meadville, PA 16335
www.christianfaithpublishing.com

Printed in the United States of America

A Question to Behold

Have you ever wondered just who God is? I mean all the respect I possibly can with this, so please don't misunderstand me. But you must admit that in your head, at least once you've asked the question, "Where did God come from?" Seriously! That's how our minds work. We're curious creatures. Since we're created beings, we can't get past the fact that God has always been and hasn't actually been created by another. I think that may be one of the main hiccups for such *intelligent* people to grasp God. He was, He is, and He will always be the Alpha and the Omega, the Beginning and End. Please just humor me for a bit.

Isaiah 40:12–18 states:

> Who has measured the waters in the hollow of His hand, measured heaven with a span and calculated the dust of the earth in a measure? Weighed the mountains in scales and the hills in a balance? Who has directed the Spirit of the Lord, or as His counselor has taught Him? With whom did He take counsel, and who instructed Him, and taught Him knowledge, and showed Him the way of understanding? Behold, the nations are as a drop in a bucket, and are counted as the small dust on the scales; look, He lifts up the isles as a very little thing. And Lebanon is not sufficient to burn, nor its beasts sufficient for a burnt offering. All nations before Him are as

nothing, and they are counted by Him less than nothing and worthless. To whom then will you liken God? Or what likeness will you compare to Him?

I can't add to the text with anything my finite mind can fathom. But I must ask the question: Who can compete with that? More than that, how could we be so fortunate to be loved by an infinite God so much that He extends unmeasurable grace and mercy such as we have under the blood covering of His Son? And He desires a relationship with us so much that He sent His only begotten Son to die in order to conquer death so we may spend eternity with Them.

As iron sharpens iron,
Just pray about it.

Apostasy

How many of you have ever doubted your salvation or know someone who has because of something done in the past? Maybe your error came after you were saved, and you condemned yourself because you figured there's no way that a born-again Christian can ever let oneself do such a thing. Or maybe you've been backslidden and think that it's all over for your relationship with God.

Can I just save you some agony and tell you that this is just not true? There's no way that God would have done what He did just to give up on you like that. Is God really that frugal to you? To start with, if you feel conviction in your heart over the reproach of your sins, then that's a good sign. That means the Holy Spirit, the great and mighty Counselor, is working on you and trying to get you to come back home. It's the one that takes the walk down the aisle to pray the sinner's prayer and to be baptized and that doesn't feel any conviction of their error who has never been saved, to begin with, but the conviction only comes from the Holy Spirit, and the Holy Spirit isn't in you if you aren't saved. So the agonizing conviction you feel is healthy!

Another situation you may find yourselves in is that you backslide for a while because you're stuck in a rut, and you think you've gone so far from God that you've reached the point of no return. And then, you let the enemy get a foothold on you, and he starts using scriptures to condemn you. Well, you're going to have to start letting Jesus answer the door when he comes knocking. Don't try to fight against him on your own because without being suited up in the whole armor of God, you won't be able to gain any ground against him; and trust me, he knows the scriptures better than any of us do. He was there every moment the Word was being written, and he does *not* mind using scriptures to make us feel condemned. Please let me remind you that any scripture can be taken out of context and be used to try and defeat us. I speak from experience. I've been there, but I'm reminded that there is *now* no condemnation for those who are in Christ Jesus (Romans 8:1).

Okay, so here you are. You've apostatized; you've backslidden. What do you do? Do you not think that God foresaw this? When Simon Peter joined Jesus's ministry, He called him a rock. Matthew 16:17–18 states, "Blessed are you, Simon Bar-Jonah, for flesh and blood has not revealed this to you, but My Father who is in heaven. And I also say to you that you are Peter, and on this rock I will build My church, and the gates of Hades shall not prevail against it." So Jesus, in this verse, was foretelling about the day of Pentecost when, after Peter, James, and John preached, five thousand were added.

Please also note: Jesus said this to Peter before He prophesied that Peter would deny Him three times before the rooster crowed that night. We all know how that went. Peter got fussy and told Jesus that he would go to death with Him, and he wound up doing just what Jesus told him he would do. Put yourself in Peter's place for a moment. He was arrogant enough that he thought he had the strength to go to death with Jesus, and when the rooster crowed on that cold empty night, it hit him: He had messed up. He denied his Savior three times! Then the next day through the chain of events that led to the horrific crucifixion of Jesus, can't you just hear Peter's words ringing in his own memory? He must've felt ashamed and worthless. So he did the only thing he knew to do. He went back to fishing with several others, returning to what he knew best, going back to what his identity was in before he put it in Christ.

But this is where it gets good! An angel comes to visit the women in Mark 16:7: "But go, tell His disciples—and Peter—that He is going before you into Galilee; there you will see Him, as He said to you." Now you see how the angel emphasized "and Peter"? But Peter was out fishing! So Jesus went to them on the shore. While they were out in the boat, pulling one of my stunts (not catching anything),

Jesus built a fire of coal, just as it was the night that Peter denied Him. In John 21, Jesus restores the disciples to His fellowship. He told them in verse 6 to cast the net on the right side of the boat, just as He did when they met. In verses 9 and 10 of 21: "Then, as soon as they had come to land, they saw a *fire of coals* there, and fish laid on it, and bread. Jesus said to them, 'Bring some of the fish which you have just caught. Come and eat breakfast' (v. 12).

So from verses 15–17, Jesus asked Peter three times if he loved Him. Why three times? Because it was three times that Peter had denied Him. But each time Peter answered, Jesus told him to feed His sheep. Jesus wasn't concerned about the apostasy he committed in the past. He knew Peter was genuinely sorrowful and repentant. So Jesus went out and met them. He met them just as He had done before in order to restore them to His ministry, to the purpose which He called them for.

If you feel that your past is in the way of your future, call out to Him, and He will meet you where you are, and He will restore you into His fellowship. And if not you but someone you know, share with them in order to restore them back into the fellowship.

As iron sharpens iron,
Just pray about it.

Are We Bold Enough?

I was reading the other day, and something really stuck out to me, but I didn't really know which way to look at it. But for some reason, listening to Dr. David Jeremiah, this thought overwhelmed me. Are we praying for boldness and opportunities to share our faith and the Gospel of Christ? How else will the unchurched hear of the saving grace that saved us?

So Paul writes in Ephesians 6:18–20:

> Praying always with all prayer and supplication in the Spirit, being watchful to this end with all perseverance and supplication for all the saints-and for me, that utterance may be given to me, that I may open my mouth boldly to make known the mystery of the gospel, for which I am an ambassador in chains; that in it I may speak boldly, as I ought to speak.

Are we praying for each other in this manner as well as ourselves? Paul, when he wrote this, was literally in chains, yet he was asking his brothers and sisters in Christ to lift him up in prayer so he would be emboldened by the Holy Spirit for others to hear the Word of God and the Gospel of Christ to be presented through him. It is necessary and imperative to pray for people to be healed, for comfort through grief, for job situations, and so forth. It is our duty to pray for that! But how many times have we stopped to pray for boldness toward each other and ourselves so that people can be reached?

To be honest with you, I haven't been praying like that! Lately, my prayer life has changed and gotten stronger, but I haven't been praying for boldness, so don't think I'm pointing fingers by no means. (If you haven't picked up on my style yet, I word my writings the way I do to provoke thought, nothing more, nothing less.) So let me ask you this. Do we hesitate to talk about *the game* or the hunt or the fishing trip? No, we don't. But we do hesitate to talk about the One who hung on the cross to bleed and die so that we may have eternal life with Him in paradise! Why? Because the world has told us that it may make someone feel uncomfortable if we talk about Him.

People can pray, just not in Jesus's name. Why? Because Jesus said that "no one comes to the Father except through Him," and the enemy knows that if we stop using His name, then we lose our power to fight against him. It would be a fool's errand to continue this life and not talk about the most important thing in this world. Luke 19:39–40 states:

> And some of the Pharisees called to Him from the crowd, "Teacher, rebuke Your disciples." But He answered and said to them, "I tell you that if these should keep silent, the stones would immediately cry out.

Jesus was telling the stiff-necked Pharisees that if every human on earth would be quiet and not call out the name "Hosanna" and praise and worship Him, then the creation would then pick up our slack and worship and praise Him. Luke 19:38 states, "Blessed is the King who comes in the name of the Lord! Peace in heaven and glory in the highest!"

If an inanimate object such as the rocks will praise the name of Jesus, shouldn't we?

> As iron sharpens iron,
> Just pray about it.

"Christianity Has No Room for Prejudice"

I've heard so many times elders in the church making sly remarks about blacks coming into the church where they worship. Who are we to decide who comes into the building where we worship the God who created all people? After all, we are the *church*, are we not? For one to deny another a place to worship due to skin color or other infractions that society looks down on is *hatred*. That right there breaks everything that we are supposed to live by. "For the two greatest commandments of all are these, 'To love the Lord your God with all your heart, soul, strength, and mind', and the other is just like it, 'To love your neighbor as yourself.'" That doesn't leave much room for prejudice, does it?

Let's look at the book of Ephesians in the second chapter. Read verses 14–20:

> For He is our peace, who made both groups one and tore down the dividing wall of hostility. [Okay, "both groups" is in reference to the Jews and Gentiles, but let's get practical: Whites and blacks or Mexicans, that's the separation most of this area.] In His flesh, He did away with the law of the commandments in regulations, so that He might create in Himself one new man from the two, resulting in peace. He did this so that He might reconcile both to God in one body

through the cross and put the *hostility* to death
by it. (vv. 14–16)

He did it to reconcile "both," not one or the other. If He did it
for both, *for all*, then why do we put stipulations on how we worship
and whom we worship with? Who do we think we are?

> When Christ came, He proclaimed the
> good news of peace to you who were far away
> and peace to those who were near. For through
> Him we both have access by one Spirit to the
> Father. So then you are no longer foreigners and
> strangers, but fellow citizens with the saints, and
> members of God's household, built on the foun-
> dation of the apostles and prophets, with Christ
> Jesus Himself as the cornerstone. (vv. 17–20)

If we (the church) are no longer foreigners and strangers to one
another, I guess that means that we can worship our Creator, sovereign God, Lord Father, and Heavenly Daddy as joint heirs and brothers, not strangers. But yet there's the ole stiff neck, fogey, *knucklehead*
that just don't want to surrender completely to the will of God. That
kind of brings to mind the letter to the church of Laodicea. What
was the warning for being lukewarm? He will spit the lukewarm out
of His mouth like vomit. If we don't give Him total control over
every aspect of our lives, are we acting lukewarm?

The derivative of the word *prejudice* is *prejudge*. To prejudge
someone before we even get a chance to know them. The book of
James talks about this as well. The second chapter of James tells us
not to show partiality toward people. It talks about the poor ver-
sus the rich I know. Just look outside the box in James the second
chapter, and it will all come back to the same principle. "Don't show
partiality, and don't show prejudice or prejudge others." In doing so,
we take it upon ourselves to choose who does and doesn't receive the
saving grace that has been bestowed upon us by our Father through

Jesus's sacrifice to save us from our sinfulness. "For we *all* fall short of the glory of God."

Who are we to discriminate? I remember as a kid this place called "Tip-Toe In." There used to be a sign above the back door "Colored Entrance." I don't much think that God hung a sign above a side door or back door reading, "Colored Entrance," to heaven.

p.s. For God so loved the *world* that He gave His only begotten Son, that whosoever believeth in Him should not perish but have everlasting life (John 3:16).

Not just us ole "country folk!"

As iron sharpens iron,
Just pray about it.

Day of Deliverance

Independence Day did not come without a price. The American Revolution took many lives as all wars do. And wars are won by equipment and skill of tactics. The way countries win wars is through technological advancement over their enemies. And that has always been true since the dawn of time.

In the days of old, many battles have been won, and many civilizations have fallen in a fight between two warriors. Take for instance the fight between David and Goliath. It started with Israel and the Philistines gathering together in battle at Sochoh. The Philistines were on a mountain on one side of the Valley of Elah, and the Israelites were on a mountain on the other side; both were in battle array and in formation ready to fight when a champion went out from the camp of the Philistines who was named Goliath. This was a beast of a man who stood 10.5 feet tall. He was suited with a bronze helmet, a chain mail coat that weighed 156 pounds, bronze armor on his legs, and a bronze javelin between his shoulders, with a long spear that had a head that weighed about nineteen pounds.

This giant challenged the Israelites to send one man out to fight him with the agreement that whichever side lost would serve the other. Territory and dominion meant everything back then, so unless one was truly confident in his victory, he wouldn't make that challenge. One can't help but sympathize with Israel in their fear after being challenged by a man of his stature, dressed in the array that Goliath was. They weren't equipped to fight him. All of Israel was of normal stature, and none of them was willing to put their life on the line, especially the potential enslavement of the entire nation forever on one duel.

But from the back came a young fellow who saw the defiance toward God that this man brought, and he didn't like it. David was, as the Bible described him, ruddy (which is fair complected) with bright eyes and good-looking. He was young and did not have the stature of a warrior. To the untrained eye, he was ill-equipped.

In 1 Samuel 17:33, it states, "And Saul said to David, 'You are not able to go against this Philistine to fight with him; for you are a youth, and he a man of war from his youth.' Isn't it like people to discourage us and sow seeds of doubt? Whether people or Satan, it's easy for us to doubt or be underestimated.

But look at David's resolve. In 1 Samuel 17:37, it states, "Moreover David said, 'The Lord, who delivered me from the paw of the lion and from the paw of the bear, He will deliver me from the hand of this Philistine.'" So we have the result of David's faith and the result of him being equipped with what the Lord gave him, and that's evidence that He will remain sovereign and keep His promises.

In 1 Samuel 17:45–47, it states:

> Then David said to the Philistine, "You come to me with a sword, with a spear, and with a javelin. But I come to you in the name of the Lord of hosts, the God of the armies of Israel, whom you have defied. This day the Lord will deliver you into my hand, and I will strike you and take your head from you. And this day I will give the carcasses of the camp of the Philistines to the birds of the air and the wild beasts of the earth, that all the earth may know that there is a God in Israel. Then all this assembly shall know that the Lord does not save with sword and spear; for the battle id the Lord's, and He will give you into our hands."

Well, things happened just as David said. The Lord gave Goliath, the champion of champions, to David, and he slew the beast merely in the name of the Lord. David knew that the stone being sent from his sling wasn't going to kill Goliath. No, it was his faith in God. Saying all that brings me to this point: Many times, I fear we bring the wrong weaponry to the battle. Hebrews 4:12 states, "For the word of God is living and powerful, and sharper than any two-edged sword, piercing even to the division of soul and spirit, and of joints and marrow, and is a discerner of the thoughts and intents of the heart."

If we can grasp that the sling of David is our prayers, and the stone of the brook is the Word of God that is "sharper than any two-edged sword," then we should be slaying the beasts of Satan on a daily basis, winning and maintaining our independence from the oppressor. We need to understand that we have victory by praying back His Word to Him, and by resisting the devil, he will flee.

As iron sharpens iron,
Just pray about it.

Do We Exercise Our Faith?

In studying Daniel chapter 6, the plot of this book gets quite deceptive. Beginning in verse 4, the officials plotted against Daniel because that's typically what happens when evil men become intimidated and jealous of God's children. So going through this chapter, they devise a plan on how to trap Daniel by attacking his faith in a way where his faith will be used or tried against him. (I encourage you to read through this as you follow along here in this devotional. Daniel 6:1–24.)

So the officials went to King Darius with their plan, and through the king's haste, not thinking mind you, he agreed to this decree. In doing so, Darius put Daniel between a rock and a hard spot. At the beginning of the chapter, we can clearly see that Darius really found favor with Daniel, so his intention was not to hurt Daniel; but by default, if Daniel were to continue in his relationship with God the Father, he was going to put himself in a bad situation with this new decree that the officials set up. This was the trap they had set. Either they would catch him not being faithful, or Daniel would subject himself to being executed.

So picking up in verse 10, Daniel, after knowing that the decree was signed, "went in his upper room with his windows open toward Jerusalem, and he knelt down on his knees three times that day and prayed and gave thanks before God, as was his custom since early days." Why didn't he just close the drapes on his windows so no one would see him? He could've waited until night or woke before everyone else so he wouldn't be seen. But if he did that, then where would be the faith?

Jesus said in Matthew 10:32–33, "Therefore whoever confesses Me before men, him I will also confess before My Father who is in heaven. But whoever denies Me before men, him I will also deny before My Father who is in heaven." You see, we each have a daily choice to either confess our Lord by our daily living or deny Him.

I struggle with things every day just like the next person, and I'm not perfect no more than anyone else, so don't think this is a message of rebuke or anything like that. We're going to mess up, but when faced with the situation to let the world know that you've surrendered your life to Christ, are you going to bear that cross or deny it?

Daniel wasn't afraid to continue his custom of praying three times a day to His holy Father. Do you think that a man in his position was praying for his selfish gain or making intercession for his beloved Jews? What if someone's only hope was for us to pray for them, but we were afraid to? What then for them?

Why wasn't Daniel afraid to continue in his prayers? He was proud to let the world know who his Father was! After all, God had revealed Himself to the entire empire on so many different occasions even just up to chapter 6. King Nebuchadnezzar had told everyone to respect the God of Daniel and his companions. King Darius did the same. Even though it doesn't say that these men had a good outcome in believing in God, they still respected who He was. Daniel knew and understood that his custom of prayer was the only way that he had strength and wisdom.

Does one face the God of heaven or Babylon? Are we to bow down to a man or to God? Do we worship idols or El Shaddai? Do we act like the heathen in order to fit in, or do we take this "relationship thing" seriously like we should and stop with the nonchalant attitude that grace is fire insurance? Do you not think that the faith as a mustard seed can actually move mountains like Jesus said it could? If that is the case, don't think that God won't hold up His end of the deal and take care of you for doing your part in glorifying Him when things get tough.

Daniel knew in his heart no matter what was to happen, God was going to see him through. King Darius, though he was sick about the whole situation, even believed that Daniel's God was going to take care of him as we read in verse 16. The text reads that God shut the mouths of the lions so they didn't just eat Daniel, but Daniel was faithful to God. God will not take care of those who are not faithful to Him, for they are His enemies. Remember, "If you deny Me before men, I will deny you before My Father who is in heaven."

Also, I'd like to point out that Satan walks about like a roaring lion seeking whom he may devour. I believe that if we seek and trust God with all our hearts, lean not on our own understanding, and in all our ways acknowledge Him, He will direct our paths (Proverbs 3:5–6).

There's a vindictive bone within my flesh that appreciates the fact that King Darius took the officials who set the trap for Daniel along with their families and killed them. But that's not right either. We should pray for our enemies and bless those who curse us, not try and seek revenge for the wrong they committed toward us. Jesus was asking God to forgive those who were torturing Him as He was dying. If He can do that, then I figure we should, at the least bit, refrain from seeking revenge.

As iron sharpens iron,
Just pray about it.

Faith Like a Babe

Matthew 11:25 states:

> At that time Jesus answered and said, "I thank You, Father, Lord of heaven and earth, that You have hidden these things from the wise and prudent and have revealed them to babes."

I open with this scripture to introduce a situation that happened to me so many years ago. My old pastor saw fit for me to get involved in children's church to start our services. He always said that if a child can't grasp the point you're trying to make, then you're overcomplicating things and have no business trying to preach it. So I went way out of my comfort zone by doing so, but the young children are most important to minister to as to fill their hearts with the love of Christ before the world teaches them the hate of the world. Jesus actually warned the people that if they were to turn a young one astray, it would be better for that person to tie a millstone around one's neck and throw themselves in the sea.

One particular Sunday morning, I was leading the children in the story coming from Matthew 14:22–33 when the disciples witnessed Jesus walking on the water. I won't type all of it down, but I encourage you to read it. For the sake of insight, the disciples were in a boat in the middle of the sea, and the winds had become really strong, and they were in some pretty rough seas. Then they looked out and saw "a Man" walking toward them, so they freaked out (just like I would've) because they thought it was a ghost. Verses 27–31 state:

> But immediately Jesus spoke to them, saying, "Be of good cheer! It is I; do not be afraid." And Peter answered Him and said, "Lord, if it is You, command me to come to You on the water." So He said, "Come." And when Peter had come down out of the boat, he walked on the water to go to Jesus. But when he saw that the wind was boisterous, he was afraid; and beginning to sink he cried out, saying, Lord, save me! And immediately Jesus stretched out His hand and caught him, and said to him, "O you of little faith, why did you doubt?"

Well, after reading the scripture, I asked my audience why they figured Peter started to sink. One young boy answered just as sincerely as could be, "Because he took his eyes off Jesus." Through the tears in my eyes, I looked around at all the mature adults in that sanctuary, and *too many* of us (me included) were surprised at the revelation of his answer.

This has two lessons wrapped up in it. The first lesson is that sometimes, in some cases, the more educated we seem to be or think we are, the less knowledgeable we actually are. Sometimes it takes the pure, undefiled heart and simple mind of a young child to understand the concepts of how faith actually works. I think as we age, unless we are raised applying our faith, we overcomplicate things to the point that we actually stop believing that Christ can actually still work miracles through us and for us.

The second lesson is that while we're doing or working on the task that God appoints us to, we will face storms, high winds, and rough seas. But if Jesus actually calls us to jump out of the boat, then we won't sink unless we start to focus more on our problems and surroundings than we do on the guidance of our Lord Jesus

Christ. Keep your eyes on Him, and we won't notice the storms around us.

> As iron sharpens iron,
> Just pray about it.

Hope

For many of you, your new year of challenges started on Monday. But for me, it was today, Wednesday, January 5, 2022, thanks to the COVID-19 experience. But today, I started thinking that a new year means new challenges, new experiences, new journeys, and hopefully for all of us, new positive goals to meet. But no matter what *new* you may be facing, God is still the same as He was last night, last year, last decade, and since the dawn of time. God was, is, and forever will be. There's nothing that will take Him by surprise! There's nothing that we will face that He hasn't already known about.

I don't know about you, but that gives me the reassurance to get up tomorrow and face another day. Each day we put behind us is another day closer to going home to glory! And on the other side of that, for the lost, it's another day closer to eternal damnation. But it's also one more day that we saw something different or had the chance to learn something new or maybe we're able to gain a new perspective on something. Just remember that the more positivity we spread and share in our day-to-day lives, the more opportunity we have of leading someone into a conversation where we can share that which our hope lies.

In 1 Peter 3:15, it states, "But sanctify the Lord God in your hearts, and always be ready to give a defense to everyone who asks you a reason for the hope that is in you, with meekness and fear." That truly is how it all should start anyway I feel. Not necessarily by preaching to them but out of their curiosity about our conduct, they confront us as to why we're so different. Then you have their interest instead of trying to figure out how to approach them. Because let's face it, there are some people who are simply unapproachable. Some people simply can't be helped because they don't want to be helped. They'll answer you with reviling and gnashing their teeth. So if simply by our good conduct we lure them into a conversation, we have the advantage.

If your year hasn't started off the way you had hoped for some reason, please be of cheer and good courage. The God of the universe cares and is there to listen and counsel you.

As iron sharpens iron,
Just pray about it.

The Deep

It totally amazes me how I can look at a certain part of scripture, and the Holy Spirit unpacks so many different lessons from just one small part! That's proof that the Scripture is living and sharper than any two-edged sword. And as you grow in the Spirit and seek to be in the presence of God, He will start to reveal things that you never saw before. Just pray as you go and "lean not on your own understanding."

But I want to direct your attention to the Gospel of Luke chapter 5. To give you some insight, the region where all this was taking place was on the northeast side of the Sea of Galilee (Lake of Gennesaret), and the primary industry was fishing. And we all can figure that commercial fishermen are always busy. There was always something to be done, and the way they fished in those days was extremely tough. And we all can understand that "fishing ain't catching." I would also like to point out that the farther you get away from the shore, the greater risk you're at to get caught up in a storm. The Sea of Galilee is about 12.5 miles tall, and at its widest point, it was roughly 7 miles wide. The wind can come out of the valley from any direction and wreak havoc on a boat.

Luke 5:1–6 states:

> So it was, as the multitude pressed about Him to hear the word of God, that He stood by the Lake of Gennesaret, and saw two boats standing by the lake; but the fishermen had gone from them and were washing their nets. Then He got

into one of the boats, which was Simon's, and asked him to put out a little from the land. And He sat down and taught the multitudes from the boat. When He had stopped speaking, He said to Simon, "Launch out into the deep and let down your nets for a catch." But Simon answered and said to Him, "Master, we have toiled all night and caught nothing; nevertheless at Your word I will let down my net." And when they had done this, they caught a great number of fish, and their net was breaking.

There are a few points I want to make from this. First and foremost, we must trust what Jesus tells us to do. If He calls you to it, He will see you through it. Second, we are called to be fishers of men just as the text tells us in verse 10. If we are to succeed in the mission and ministry that God has called us to, we must launch into the deep no matter how frightening the waters are. We will never become fishers of men if we stay on the shore where it's safe. We must prepare ourselves to get out of our comfort zones.

As iron sharpens iron,
Just pray about it.

Justified by Faith

I was journaling in the third chapter of Romans where Paul is beginning to explain the theology of our justification through our faith in Jesus Christ. I couldn't help but reflect on how He has shown me much grace through all my foolishness. But as I came across Romans 3:23 where it says (and I know y'all can quote it), "All have *sinned, and fall* short of the glory of God." I couldn't help but pay attention to something. Something I never thought about before.

Take a look at those two words for a minute. The word *sinned* is in the past tense (have sinned) because we have, all, in the past sinned, which means we have transgressed against the divine boundary between good and evil. Well, that being said, *fall* is in the present tense. Search your heart on this matter and ask Him about this.

Romans 3:24–28 states:

> Being justified freely by His grace through the redemption that is in Christ Jesus, whom God set forth as a propitiation by His blood, through faith, to demonstrate His righteousness, because in His forbearance God had passed over the sins that were previously committed, to demonstrate at the present time His righteousness, that He might be just and the justifier of the one who has faith in Jesus. Where is boasting then? It is excluded. By what law? Of works? No, but by the law of faith. Therefore we conclude that a man is justified by faith apart from the deeds of the law.

The second part of verse 25 quotes, "Sins that were previously committed." Once we've confessed our sins with our mouths and believe in our hearts that Jesus came, died, and was raised in order to pay for our sins, past, present, and future, it's at that moment that we are redeemed; and all our actions are justified, not of works but by faith. And we can conclude, as Paul writes in verse 28, that man is justified by faith apart from the deeds of the law, which means that we can't earn with deeds our salvation. This also means that after we are in Christ, there is nothing that we can do to where we will be snatched from His hands.

This whole time we stumble and "fall short," Satan is grumbling to God about all we are doing wrong; but Jesus, who sits at the right hand of the Father as our supreme advocate, tells God our Father that we have been justified by believing in His sacrifice and that we belong to Him. This isn't fire insurance so we can do as we want. If one is truly saved, they'll feel conviction from their trespasses and won't want to live in sin anyway. Even being backslidden, there are feelings that are hard to live with.

As iron sharpens iron,
Just pray about it.

New for the Year

With the new year approaching, I can't help but reflect on things in the past year. I do this every year though I haven't done anything about it in the past, just ponder on it. But I do look at it in regard to things I want to be different next year. But if you look at things from that angle, then you must ask what you're going to change in your life for things to be different. After all, to have a different outcome, there must be changes made, right?

It comes to a point that each of us as individuals has to not only figure out what changes need to be made, but we must also have the integrity to see those changes through. For quite a while, that's where I have failed. I failed to find the integrity within myself to make the changes I know I needed to make. I challenged my family this year to make a list of things they want to be different this coming year and to implement a plan on how to make those changes come to pass. After all, it's up to us to change the world, right? But no matter when this is read, whether read as it is sent out, or in the middle of the year, or even two years from now, you don't have to wait for a new year to make new changes. That's why I don't care for "new year's resolutions."

If you feel that you need to make changes in your life, first figure out what you need to change, then assess how much resistance these changes will be met with so you can prepare accordingly, then devise a plan on how to change, and finally, pray for the integrity to stick to your plan of change. Be mindful that sometimes small changes will take a while to manifest, but in the end, it is very well worth it. Jeremiah 29:11–14 states:

> For I know the thoughts that I think toward you, says the Lord, thoughts of peace and not of evil, to give you a future and a hope. Then you will call upon Me and go and pray to Me, and I will listen to you. And you will seek Me and find Me, when you search for Me with all your heart. I will be found by you, says the Lord, and I will bring you back from your captivity; I will gather you from all the nations and from all the places where I have driven you, says the Lord, and I will bring you to the place from which I cause you to be carried away captive.

Try to parallel your life with that of Israel. Here, God is talking to His people through His prophet Jeremiah. If you read further into the text both forward and behind, you'll see that Israel is in captivity under the rule of Babylon. They were in captivity because they fell away from God and lost God's protection. When you live in sin (not just commit a sin and then repent of it), God will not honor your disobedience. Parallel that with their captivity. Sin equals captivity, for you're captive to whatever draws you away and entices you. The faraway nations equal your distance from God due to your sinful lifestyle.

Also notice that in every Old Testament situation where God removed His protective hedge from around Israel, it was so that His children would repent of their sins and come back to Him for His protection and guidance. Though in some cases things are different now than they were back then, remember Jesus said that He did not come to abolish the law but to fulfill it. I don't think that things are so different as much as our perception of the way things are.

I would like to put each of you to a challenge if you're up to it: Make a list of just a few things that will make your life better in 2022. Maybe goals that you've wanted to set but didn't know how you could. Bad habits you know you need to drop or maybe stagnant habits that you think you need to replace with new vibrant ones that will make your life better. Take it one step at a time. Let's start a revival among our small group! That's how forest fires start you know, by one single ember! I also ask for y'all to hold my feet to the fire with this too. We all need an accountability partner. Let's make a difference in the next year to the people we interact with outside church. Let's start something so drastic by one change at a time that God will say, "Well done, My good and faithful servant," and Satan will get nervous at the mere thought of what's happening!

Isaiah 43:18–19 states:

> Do not remember the former things, nor consider the things of old. Behold, I will do a new thing, now it shall spring forth; shall you not know it? I will even make a road in the wilderness and rivers in the desert.

As iron sharpens iron,
Just pray about it.

Our Ministry

Let's say that you were approached one day by someone whom you actually have a fair amount of interaction with, and they asked about salvation and getting saved. What would be your initial reaction? Would you get all excited and try to set up a meeting with your pastor? Would you wish them good luck with their journey and tell them that you'll be praying for them? Would you lock up in fear that you would be asked some really tough questions that you may get wrong? After all, we don't want to answer any serious questions wrong! I mean, how could someone answer questions about salvation if they know that they sin themselves? "How dare a *hypocrite* be so bold as to try and help someone understand salvation." What does our own salvation mean to us if we still fall short of the glory of God? Are "church folk" even prepared enough to help someone find their salvation, just simple ole church folk that doesn't have any theology degree or ministerial licensing, or formal education? Well, what if you can't really think of the right scripture passage at the right time, or you don't really read very well in front of people and don't want to be embarrassed?

Jesus went through the most excruciatingly painful death so that the world could have a personal relationship with the Father, and that relationship, being so special and personal, should prompt us to *want* to share our faith with others and to be ready to lead someone to a relationship with the Savior. Now I will say that yes, we should be concerned about answering questions wrongly. That's why it's up to us to test the spirits and to learn what the Word says, not what people tell us what the Word says.

In those regards, how do you get to know someone? Let's take for example the ones in your life whom you call friends. How did you get to the point where you felt comfortable calling them friends? You spent time with them and learned their character traits and their disposition and their heart. A relationship isn't about what that person can do for you. It's about compatibility, and it's about common ground. But you won't know any of that unless you spend time with that person.

Jesus has already done more for us all than we could possibly ever do in return for Him, so why don't we spend time getting to know Him and trust Him as we should? Why don't we prepare ourselves for that moment when we get to introduce someone to Him? In 1 Peter 3:15, it states, "But sanctify the Lord God in your hearts, and always be ready to give a defense to everyone who asks you a reason for the hope that is in you, with meekness and fear."

It's awesome to want to bring someone to your pastor, but is your faith in the pastor? It's wonderful to bring someone to your church and get them plugged in, but is your faith in the assembly? It's great to admit that you don't have all the answers, but are you going to let that stop you from witnessing to someone and walking them through the first steps toward their salvation? Could you lead someone in the sinner's prayer?

I think that we need to prepare for those certain times. You never know when you may have that opportunity to not just make a difference in someone's life but be that guiding light that leads someone out of darkness and into salvation. Granted we can't do anything without the Holy Spirit anyway. We can't save anyone! It's the blood of Jesus Christ that saves us, not us or any power or authority of ourselves. But He wants us to be a part of it. After all, we are the body of Christ. So are the arms reaching? Are the hands healing? Are the feet running toward righteousness? Is the mouth speaking the truth? In evangelical teaching, the Roman road to salvation is Romans 3:23, 6:23, and 10:9–10 and Ephesians 2:8–9; and it's relative to share 1 John 1:8–10.

As iron sharpens iron,
Just pray about it.

Prepare Yourself

It doesn't take a genius to analyze ancient texts and figure out that we are living in the last days. But there isn't anyone who can predict the end of the age though people have tried. There have been goofballs who have said that they know when the return of Christ is going to happen, so you need to buy your ticket from them. Y2K was pretty crazy too! People went out and bought all kinds of expensive cars, trucks, off-road toys, and the like, thinking they wouldn't have to pay for them; and things didn't turn out the way they thought and were stuck with it. And then the talk about the north and south poles switching, which in turn will cause something catastrophic. Let's not forget about global warming and so on and so forth.

Let me give you some hope against all this garbage. Matthew 24:35–36 states:

> Heaven and earth will pass away, but My words will by no means pass away. But of that day and hour no one knows, not even the angels of heaven, but My Father only. But as the days of Noah were, so also will the coming of the Son of Man be.

Notice that every piece of text that I copy out of the Bible, I copy just as my Bible reads it, and this text is written in red. Jesus said, "But My Father only." No man on earth, no matter how smart he is, will be able to predict neither the end of the world nor the rapture of the church nor anything else. There are signs given to us in

Matthew 24, all through Daniel, Isaiah, Ezekiel, and most assuredly in Revelation that help explain things so we can be better prepared. We were given warning signs of bad times to come, but no one knows the day that will take claim to civilization as we know it.

Let me stress the importance of keeping a level head in any time of crisis. Jesus told us in Matthew 6 not to worry. Actually, in my Bible, Matthew 6 beginning in verse 25 is titled "the cure for worry." I believe that to worry is to sin because we show by worrying that we have no faith in God to take care of us. Saying that, let me say this: Start working on a food pantry for your family, as well as a thirty-day water supply and a water filter, for when the water runs out or for the happenstance of some of your water becoming contaminated.

The way to calculate the water is a gallon per person per day. And as far as the food, I'm still working on all that. I'm not trying to strike fear in anyone, nor do I want to come off as some psycho doomsday prepper. But we need to be prepared for bad times ahead. Hosea 4:6 states, "My people are destroyed for lack of knowledge." Never mind a doomsday apocalypse! What when another major hurricane hits the Gulf Coast or Atlantic, and the food supplies are cut off (again), and the fuel goes into shortage (again)? Or what if the Midwest faces a severe drought, and they can't grow hay for livestock? That spells famine.

We must prepare ourselves physically for bad times ahead. But most importantly, we must prepare our hearts and the hearts of our loved ones for a time of spiritual famine when our freedoms are stripped away by our governors, and we're told we can't worship the King of kings anymore. The day is coming, my beloved, so prepare yourselves. This principle or thought has nothing to do with living in fear but everything about heeding certain warnings and preparing for hard times. That's all.

As iron sharpens iron,
Just pray about it.

Salt of the Earth

What does your salvation mean to you? Is it fire insurance? Is it simply your ticket to heaven and out of hell? How do you view yourself as a Christian? Most importantly, how do you think you are *supposed* to be to the rest of the world? Well, I'll give you a break from questions for a bit, and I'll tell you what we, as Christians, are supposed to be to the rest of the world or rather show you what Jesus says about it. Matthew 5:13–16 states:

> You are the salt of the earth; but if the salt loses its flavor, how shall it be seasoned? It is then good for nothing but to be thrown out and trampled underfoot by men. You are the Light of the world. A city that is set on a hill cannot be hidden. Nor do they light a lamp and put it under a basket, but on a lampstand, and it gives light to all who are in the house. Let your light so shine before men, that they may see your good works and glorify your Father in heaven.

We are no doubt saved by grace through faith in Christ Jesus, and it is not of works, lest anyone should boast (Ephesians 2:8–9). We can't earn our salvation by works, but we can't express our faith without working for the kingdom either! We are supposed to be the salt of the earth, but do you actually understand what it means to be the salt of the earth?

Salt is used for seasoning bland food, and it burns open cuts and helps heal sore muscles. Salt also preserves food, and it keeps bugs away. And that just names a few. So how does that relate to us? We are to live a life that means to preserve truth, truth being the infallible Word of God just as food. Remember that Jesus told Satan that man can't live off of bread alone but by every Word of God? We are to be a therapeutic reaction to help heal the sick, physically sick as well as spiritually sick. And in a raw world that is cut to the core, we are to be a burning irritant as we share the love of Christ!

It isn't for the faint of heart, mind you, but it is what we're supposed to do. But we are not just to be the salt of the earth; we are also called to be the light burning in the dark. When I read this part of the passage, it makes me think of a lighthouse on the shoreline up on a hill where there's a vantage point. The lighthouse is set in a place high above, then built to be pretty tall in order to broadcast the light to warn the ships that they're nearing imminent danger. Typically, you think of sharp rocks and shallow surf that spell certain disaster for a ship.

When we become saved, we have been consumed by the burning fire of the Holy Spirit, which produces such a light that can't be mistaken! Who, in their right mind, would hide that light? You may think to yourself that "you don't hide the light within you," yet people can't tell you apart. What about the jesting on your job that you know isn't honoring God? If you fall in there instead of walking away, then you suppress that light. If you let your negative side control your emotions and actions instead of being positive and looking at things as being half full, then you suppress the light within you.

The most terrifying thing about suppressing or hiding the light is that we can't warn the lost people of the dangerous rocks and snares that they are heading for. Well, friend, we are responsible for leading the lost in the way of righteousness. Ezekiel chapters 3 and 33 talk about the watchman on the wall. I won't go into that, but I encourage you to read it. Read those chapters and pray about what they are saying. We are held accountable for the people we lead astray by our unrighteous actions as well as people we don't minister to for the sake of suppressing the light that is within us. Let's do better as a group and individuals to reach a lost and dying world by being the salt of the earth and the light of the world!

As iron sharpens iron,
Just pray about it.

Separation

I've had some shortcomings in the past couple of weeks as a new job had me preoccupied, busy, and distracted; and I really started beating myself up over it. And my mind went straight to the scriptures that the beloved Paul wrote:

> For what I am doing, I do not understand. For what I will to do, that I do not practice; but what I hate, that I do. If then, I do what I will not to do, I agree with the law that it is good. But now, it is no longer I who do it, but sin that dwells in me. For I know that in me (that is in my flesh) nothing good dwells; for to will is present with me, but how to perform what is good I do not find. (Romans 7:15–18)

> O wretched man that I am! Who will deliver me from this body of death? I thank God through Jesus Chris our Lord! So then, with the mind, I myself serve the law of God but with the flesh the law of sin. (Romans 7:24–25)

It's my heartfelt belief that when we fall short, one of two things will happen. Either we will feel wretched and distant and feel the weight of the shame, or we won't feel anything at all. If we don't feel anything at all, then the Spirit of God *does not* live inside of us! If we do feel the shame, then that's the Holy Spirit convicting us and tugging at us, telling us that we must repent of that and come back to the Father in fellowship.

Okay, but what about the feeling of separation? Sin separates us from the fellowship with El Elyon (the Most High God). When Jesus was hung on the cross to bear all our shame, there was a separation between Him and the Father God because God is so holy and pure that He cannot look on sin. Well, that's why our Lord Jesus Christ was there—to bear all our sin and shame. Everything that happened on the hill of Calvary was a series of symbolic events between Jesus Christ and God our Heavenly Father (El Shaddai)! Please read this next sentence as many times as you need for it to sink in. Though it took place between Them, *it was for us!* And Jesus's arms were stretched out, and nails pierced His flesh to show the world that He separated our sins from us as far as the east is from the west! And when the sky turned black from the absence of the sun, that represented God turning His back toward Jesus. He cried out in agony, "Eli, Eli, lama sabachthani?" "My God, My God, why has Thou forsaken Me?"

His agony wasn't due to the physical pain! His agony came from the distance He felt between Him and the Father! Then the veil was torn to give us *direct* access to El Elyon so we wouldn't have to go through a corrupt priesthood and offer any more sacrifices for our atonement.

Jesus was that ultimate atonement for our sins. He did what He did so we wouldn't have to feel separated anymore! He became the supreme advocate, standing at the right hand of the Father, so when you stand before the throne in judgment (if you have accepted Him as your Savior), He will give account for you and tell the Holy Judge that your sins are *paid in full!*

So, beloved, it is important that you feel shame for falling short, but it's more important for you to understand that there is now no condemnation for those who are in Christ Jesus as it says in Romans 8:1. Grace isn't fire insurance, so we must strive constantly to stay in the fellowship with Christ. Notice I didn't say, "strive to do better," right? We can't be good enough on our own, so quit trying. You'll never work your way into heaven. It's not about earning our way anywhere. It's about having a relationship with God through Jesus with the Holy Spirit. And if we are in Christ, then we live with this promise:

> Who shall separate us from the love of Christ? Shall tribulation, or distress, or persecution, or famine, or nakedness, or peril, or sword? As it is written; For Your sake, we are killed all day long; we are accounted as sheep for the slaughter. Yet in all these things we are more than conquerors through Him who loved us. For I am persuaded that neither death nor life, nor angels nor principalities nor powers, nor things present nor things to come nor height nor depth, nor any other created thing, shall be able to separate us from the love of God which is in Christ Jesus our Lord. (Romans 8:35–39)

> As iron sharpens iron,
> Just pray about it.

Sin, the Problem of the Flesh

Why do people battle with sin day after day? Though we don't want to admit this problem, sin is alive and ever present. I wish with every ounce of my being that sin wasn't a factor, but thanks to Adam and Eve, they surrendered their authority of the earth to Satan. And he is the master of deception. Anything he can do to get the Christians off balance and knock us off our feet, he's gonna do it. There's one thing that we must realize about his strategy: It creeps up on you. It is, no doubt, a slow fade. He won't attack at full force to start with because that would be too obvious to us as to what's going on. He slowly and quietly sneaks up on us.

Sin starts off as a simple thought, moving on to a temptation, growing stronger into a desire that we can't ignore which manifests, and taking control of us, at least until we call on Jesus and give Him back control. Satan knows that sin causes separation of fellowship between us and God, so he's working constantly, with his minions, to put anything and everything he can in our way to cause us to stumble and fall. It's just as if we're walking around in the dark, tripping over things. That's why we must do everything we can to walk in the light. If he can get us down, then we are weak and subject to those temptations.

In 1 John 1:5–6, it states, "God is light and in Him is no darkness at all. If we say that we have fellowship with Him, and walk in darkness, we lie and do not practice the truth." Stumbling over something and living in sin is a bit different in that when you live in sin, you won't produce any good fruit for the kingdom of Christ; but when you stumble, that's just it—you stumble and get back up and on track toward Him and mission for Him. Neither one is great, but only one will have long-term effects on your inner spirit and your mission. When you are living in sin, you're walking in darkness and are separated from fellowship with Abba Father.

I'm at constant war with a law that's within, and everything in me can't figure it out. Romans 7:14–25 states:

> For we know that the law is spiritual, but I am carnal, sold under sin. For what I am doing, I do not understand. For what I will to do, that I do not practice; but what I hate, that I do. If, then, I do what I will not to do, I agree with the law that it is good. But now, it is no longer I who do it, but sin that dwells in me. For I know that in me (that is, in my flesh) nothing good dwells; for to will is present with me, but how to perform what is good I do not find. For the good that I will to do, I do not do; but the evil I will not to do, that I practice. Now if I do what I will not to do, it is no longer I who do it, but sin that dwells in me. I find then a law, that evil is present with me, the one who wills to do good. For I delight in the law of God according to the inward man. But I see another law in my members, warring against the law of my mind, and bringing me into captivity to the law of sin which is in my members. O wretched man that I am! Who will deliver me from this body of death? I thank God—through Jesus Christ our Lord! So then, with the mind I myself serve the law of God, but with the flesh the law of sin.

But it's not hopeless for us, beloved. We're not the first generation to deal with this! Paul, in his intellect, struggled with this, but he overcame it. In 1 John 1:9, it states, "If we confess our sins,

He is faithful and just to forgive us our sins and cleanse us from all unrighteousness."

As iron sharpens iron,
Just pray about it.

Stewardship

What do you think that stewardship is exactly? When you hear that word, what emotions or thoughts are triggered? For me (and I'm sure for many of you), I was raised up learning how to use words without necessarily knowing the definition. That's the case a lot for me. But stewardship is defined as "the job of supervising or taking care of something, such as an organization or property" which I actually had the jest of this word meaning and the concept of it as well. But through a conversation with an elder lady a day or so before, she said something that really made me stop and think about whether I took this to heart. Many times, when people obtain a property of any sort, they pray a blessing over it in thanking God for blessing them with it, and they earnestly have in their hearts to use it to glorify God with it. That's being a good steward of the gift. When we tithe with our income, we pray to the Lord to teach us to be good stewards and to bless and multiply our offerings. When we do that, we acknowledge the fact that God has let us use His resources, and we're simply giving back as a form of worship in order to honor Him.

But what about our time? Are we good stewards of our time? That really hit me like a brick when my conversation turned to that. It started with the topic of social media. She was talking about how she had to get off Facebook due to people just acting foolish and telling all their business there, so she got tired of it and deactivated her account. That led me to share that I deactivated my social media accounts as well (which I shared the other day). Then she told me that she has to watch how much time she spends on things as simple as making baskets instead of spending time with God in the Word. And when she said that, it really sank in and provoked my feelings.

Am I being a good steward of the "borrowed time" that I get from God? One thing I'm struggling with is the fact that I spend so much time away from my family due to my job. I have to work. We all have to work. The Bible says that he who does not work does not eat. Working is being a good steward of the talents and abilities that God has given us. But do I make the most of my free time and the time when I'm home? I honestly don't think I do a good enough job with that.

Let me go back to the "borrowed time" comment. Because that's all it is. We all know that we are not promised tomorrow. At any given moment, our life could be over. To be honest with you, I've often wondered, *When I'm gone, how will people remember me? Will my family know how much I love them, and will God meet me and say, "Well done, thy good and faithful servant"?* That sometimes haunts me.

In 1 Peter 4:7–10, it states:

> But the end of all things is at hand; therefore, be serious and watchful in your prayers. And above all things have fervent love for one another, for "love will cover a multitude of sins." Be hospitable to one another without grumbling. As each one has received a gift, minister it to one another, as good stewards of the manifold grace of God.

As iron sharpens iron,
Just pray about it.

Support the Shepherd

The times we are living are exceedingly tough and will continue to get tougher. I hate to be the bearer of bad news, but it really is no secret since we have been warned about it. Look at the toll that the COVID-19 ordeal placed on the local church. Look at all the Christian persecution across the world and around here. Pastors are being gagged (figuratively speaking) to the point that they face severe punishment for preaching the Truth. We all know whether we want to accept it or not that Christianity isn't just dying off but being murdered.

The church that Jesus died to establish is being silenced, forced into hiding, broken apart, scattered into exile, martyred, and even broken apart from within. Here in America, we deal with enough challenges in our day-to-day lives; and sooner than later, I fear that we will face what Christians in the far corners of the world are facing, so we all need to make our minds up about how we're going to handle it. Ask yourself, When times really get hard and you face persecution, will you stand firm in your faith, or will you buckle under pressure? Will you choose to stand firm in your faith when you're faced with certain death? What will we do for our leadership? If our spiritual leaders fall under attack, will we stand behind them? Do we stand behind and beside our church leaders now?

I've been burdened by this in the past and wrote a short devotional from this passage. But it brings me under conviction now, more so than ever before, since the times are so threatening. Do I let my pastor know that I am there to lift him up? If the churches across our nation did a better job at that, would we see a better outcome in the battle against our enemy?

Exodus 17:9–13 states:

> And Moses said to Joshua, "choose us some men and go out, fight with Amalek. Tomorrow I will stand on the top of the hill with the rod of God in my hand." So Joshua did as Moses said to him, and fought with Amalek. And Moses, Aaron, and Hur went up to the top of the hill. And so it was, when Moses held up his hand, that Israel prevailed; and when he let down his hand, Amalek prevailed. But Moses' hands became heavy; so they took a stone and put it under him, and he sat on it. And Aaron and Hur supported his hands, one on one side, and the other on the other side; and his hands were steady until the going down of the sun. So Joshua defeated Amalek and his people with the edge of the sword.

Okay, say Moses represents our pastor (interim or full-time doesn't matter), and Joshua and the army of Israel represent us. Amalek and his army represent Satan and his minions and the sword represent the Word of God, which is sharper than any two-edged sword, piercing even to the division of soul and spirit and of joints and marrow and is a discerner of the thoughts and intents of the heart (Hebrews 4:12). If we study this, we can draw a parallel between ourselves and the Old Testament Israel.

Moses couldn't, by himself, hold his hands up for the amount of time needed for Joshua's army to gain a victory. It required some companions to help support him in order for his hands to remain lifted up. It's no different from the laying on of hands to cover someone with the blessings of God. That's what Moses was doing. But he couldn't do it alone.

Our pastors today can't do it alone either. This comes as a three-fold lesson. The pastor needs faithful supporters to help hold him up and to know that he can't do it alone, and out of each congregation, there must be a band of believers that are willing to rally around that anointed man of God and continually bathe him in prayer. Not only in their quiet time but also to let him know that they are there for him. It's only half of it to pray for him. We must not hesitate to love and openly pray over him; that way, he feels that support.

As iron sharpens iron,
Just pray about it.

The Body of Christ

Let me open this with a scripture. In 1 Corinthians 12:12–13, it states:

> For as the body is one and has many members, but all the members of that one body, being many, are one body, so also is Christ. For by one Spirit we were all baptized into one body-whether Jews or Greeks, whether slaves or free—and have all been made to drink into one Spirit.

Do we not realize that we, as a Church family, are the body of Christ and far more than just a social group that meets on certain days of the week? We are members of the heavenly family that Jesus died to obtain. If in fact you are baptized in the baptism of Jesus Christ, you are far more than just dust in the wind. We all are called according to His purpose if indeed; we have answered that calling and given ourselves over to His lordship and quit living for our own selfish desires. And as the body of Christ, we all are set apart with special gifts and talents. We each have certain abilities that others don't have, and each of us has certain gifted attributes that are quite unique. But do we go through life living out this truth?

We all have jobs, right? We go to work to earn wages in order to provide for our families. Within those jobs, we have certain talents and trade skills that help us move up along the way in our jobs. But for many of us, we tend to live as if that's where it stops. Then come Sunday, we head to church to socialize for a bit and go through the motions and get a little *feel-good* or whatever. But we don't share our talents and gifts with others. We don't incorporate those attributes into our part of worship.

What if I told you that in order to worship the King of kings, you have to do more than just show up at the appointed time of the meeting, drop your tithe on the offering plate, sing a few songs, then go home? It takes so much more than just that, for He did so much more for us! HE gave the ultimate sacrifice to buy our ransom, so don't you think we owe Him more than what we're giving Him?

Now let me just say that if you're diligently working behind the scenes to make things happen at your assembly, then you should know this isn't for you! But there's no secret that there are too many church members who aren't doing their part for various reasons, and we need to right this wrong. I'm willing to put myself out there and say that many people feel inadequate, and this is a problem that I think, by default, we may have created.

In this world, we have major pride issues going both ways, too much pride or not enough to see your own worth. It's our responsibility as the body of Christ to get people past that. It's all problems that stem from brokenness, and that's what we are supposed to do: Through the guidance of the Holy Spirit, minister to and help heal the broken people.

In 1 Corinthians 12:21–27, it states:

> And the eye cannot say to the hand, "I have no need of you"; nor again the head to the feet, "I have no need of you." No, much rather, those members of the body which seem to be weaker are necessary. And those members of the body which we think to be less honorable, on these we bestow greater honor; and our unpresentable parts have greater modesty, but our presentable parts have no need. But God composed the body, having given greater honor to that part which lacks it, that there should be no schism in the body, but that the members should have the same

care for one another. And if one member suffers,
all the members suffer with it; or if one member is honored, all the members rejoice with it.
Now you are the body of Christ, and members
individually.

Beloved, we are the body of Christ Jesus! We are the church of
Christ Jesus! We need to start living like it now more so than at any
other time in our existence. It's time for us to start living with a purpose. As the redeemed children of God, we have a lot of lost people
to seek after, many in our own assemblies. But we must communi-
cate with the other members of the body to obtain direction. For if
the feet are trying to go in different directions, nothing will ever get
accomplished.

As iron sharpens iron,
Just pray about it.

The Spiritual High

Have you ever stopped to take a moment to really think about Moses's encounter with God on top of Mount Sinai? At that moment in his life, Moses was probably the closest he would be or ever had been to God. Exodus 34:29–30 states that Moses came down from Mount Sinai, and his face shone.

> Now it was so, when Moses came down from Mount Sinai (and the two tablets of the Testimony were in Moses's hand when he came down from the mountain), that Moses did not know that the skin of his face shone while he talked with Him. So when Aaron and all the children of Israel saw Moses, behold, the skin of his face shone, and they were afraid to come near him.

Why did Moses's face shine? It was because the Spirit of God illuminated his face. That's how close Moses was to God. Talk about being on a spiritual high! That's the way it feels to be in the center of God's will. One can almost feel the Spirit illuminate them. There's one issue about all of this. Moses didn't stay on Mount Sinai. He had to come down some time or another. Why did Moses come down? He had in his hands something that was very valuable, something that he was charged by the Holy of holies to deliver to His chosen people. The Testimony of God's Word was the Law of God (the Commandments). Moses had to come down in order to bring the

Word of God to the people. Moses went up because not everyone was capable. Moses was His elect for that specific task; no one else was called.

He had a specific job to do, and he not only had to get in the closeness of God to receive the Word, but he also had to come down to deliver the Word to the people. So we have the spiritual high, the decent, and the delivery. Let's focus on the descent for a moment. It's like hitting rock bottom when you come off of a spiritual high. It truly is bittersweet. It has to be done, but it sure is hard. Why is the descent so important? Once you're enlightened, all you should be doing is trying your best to share the love of Christ through the Word. That's the delivery. But first, you have to take that decent to where the carnally minded are (not to be of the world but to be *in* the world).

It's our mandate to share with others the Truth. If we're floating around on cloud nine, then we won't be able to reach the ones who just flat-out don't understand. I'm not saying that we're not supposed to be imitators of Christ. And I'm not saying that we're supposed to act like the carnal either. What I am saying is that in order to be able to minister/witness to the lost/carnal, we must be broken for them. We must be sympathetic. And that requires being, not on the mountaintop but also in the valley beside them.

Okay, stay with me, "spiritual high (where we are in the closeness with God when we receive the Word to be shared), decent (when we come off of our spiritual high), and delivery (when we reach out to the lost and minister to them through Word, and love, in order to deliver His message)." How do we receive a spiritual high? A "spiritual high" comes from seeking the face of God, to be in the center of His will. And when you find yourself in the center of God's will, then there won't be any distractions; hence, you will hear the Word of God speak to you like no other way at no other time imaginable.

> As iron sharpens iron,
> Just pray about it.

The Stumbling Block

There are many things we may find ourselves doing that are not necessarily sinful by any order we may find in the Bible, but there's something we must realize. If things we do lead others to stumble due to a misunderstanding or lack of knowledge on their part, then we will be held accountable for that. That puts things into perspective for me.

Thinking about this takes me back to a conversation that I had with a young man actually in the midst of my self-given challenge to quit drinking. Basically, that young man, as well as a couple of others, was going to get a bite to eat one evening after work; and it came around the topic of me getting some drinks that night, and I made the comment: "There's more to what I need to be doing than just keeping down this path. I have to do better and quit drinking because though the Bible doesn't say anything about drinking being a sin if I continue in it and lead someone else astray, then their falling short will be imputed as a sin against me."

He asked me what I meant, and I said, "If my drinking shows people a bad influence, then I'll be held accountable for that." From my gathering, that was a turning point for him as well as me. Praise be unto God for that!

Well, let's get practical for a bit. Is drinking the only way that Christians can fall short and be a stumbling block for someone to trip over? No, it's not! There are several ways that we can mess up and lead someone astray. Telling dirty jokes, acting vulgar toward the opposite sex, being negative all the time, complaining about every little thing, being arrogant, treating people poorly, using foul language as normal vocabulary, and so forth are but a few.

I know that these on the list don't take much to frown on and are quite apparently sinful in nature; there are just what I came up with at a whim. There are many subtler things that we tend to do that really aren't considered a sin but can and will cause a new believer to stumble. Just give yourself a good evaluation and see what the Holy Spirit convicts you about. We all fall short, and there's no time like now to make positive changes to correct the error. Ask yourself this question: Do we consider the small things when it comes to trying to remove stumbling blocks? We need to be mindful of what we do that poses the risk of causing others to stumble, right? Matthew 18:6 states, "But whoever causes one of these little ones who believe in Me to sin, it would be better for him if a millstone were hung around his neck, and he were drowned in the depth of the sea."

Yes, Jesus was speaking of the young children in His presence. But do you think this disqualifies an adult who is a babe in Christ who is new to the faith and trying to learn or, simply enough, one whom we should try and minister to and befriend?

Romans 14:15–19 states:

> Yet if your brother is grieved because of your food, you are no longer walking in love. Do not destroy with your food the one for whom Christ died. Therefore do not let your good be spoken of as evil; for the kingdom of God is not eating and drinking, but righteousness and peace and joy in the Holy Spirit. For he who serves Christ in these things is acceptable to God and approved by men. Therefore let us pursue the things which make for peace and the things by which one may edify another.

I don't mean to take this out of context by any means, so I'll give you a quick rundown: Paul was addressing customary ordinances concerning the clean dietary rituals of the different people.

It's no secret that people in the east don't eat pork meat. (During lent, Catholics don't eat meat on Fridays.) Though I'm not trying to take this out of context, how would it apply to us if we take the whole diet thing out of the equation and add in there different things that we've listed earlier? If we take the concept of "costumary eating" out and simply replaced this with different things that, though isn't considered a sin, cause our neighbor to stumble, the effect is still the same.

We should be mindful of these things to grow in our faith and be a living testimony as well as an ambassador for God's holy kingdom. Whatever sacrifices we must make to reach a dying world and to strengthen the babes in Christ, we need to strive to do.

As iron sharpens iron,
Just pray about it.

The Vinedresser

John 15:1–8 states:

> I AM the true vine, and My Father is the vinedresser. Every branch in Me that does not bear fruit He takes away; and every branch that bears fruit He prunes, that it may bear more fruit. You are already clean because of the word which I have spoken to you. Abide in Me, and I in you. As the branch cannot bear fruit of itself, unless it abides in the vine, neither can you, unless you abide in Me. I am the vine, you are the branches. He who abides in Me, and I in him, bears much fruit; for without Me you can do nothing. If anyone does not abide in Me, he is cast out as a branch and is withered; and they gather them and throw them into the fire, and they are burned. If you abide in Me, and My words abide in you, you will ask what you desire, and it shall be done for you. By this My Father is glorified, that you bear much fruit; so you will be My disciples.

If you haven't wondered about growing grapes or muscadines, then you should do some research on what it takes to grow a strong productive grapevine (in order for this to make sense). For the first year, you cut all buds, shoots, and canes off of the vine as you train it to grow upward. This is so that all nutrition will go into the vine, allowing it to grow at its max potential. For the second year, you allow the vine to let canes run outward, but you still must keep all the fruit buds and shoots pruned off. For the third year, you let it do its thing, but you still prune selectively in wintertime. If you let the old growth linger, then that old growth will take nutrients from the new potential fruit production. Every year, you'll want to spend some time with your grapevines and love on 'em a bit so your harvest will be plentiful.

As we are received by Christ into the heavenly family, we are expected to come as we are. No qualifications to meet. No tests to take for acceptance. We are to come broken, humbled, wretched, dirty sinners. Sinners who know we need a Savior that has paid the price for our freedom from the bondage of sin. That being said, we must understand that we have much to let go of.

Everyone has things that they must let go of. We can't do it alone, nor are we expected to. But as the process takes place, we must allow Him to do His work in us. We must be prepared to let the Vinedresser prune all the unnecessary growth from our lives. We are all expected to produce fruit in our everyday lives, loving the people in this lost and dying world, loving them by sharing the "good news" of Christ's redeeming blood.

Remember, hell was *not* created for people. "It is appointed unto man once to die then the judgment" (Hebrews 9:27). We are commissioned when we are saved to witness as many lost people as we can, and that is the fruit that we are to produce. We can't produce fruit if we let overgrowth choke out our testimonies. And it is your testimony that will show proof of the works of the Holy Spirit in your life. But you can't have a testimony if you're still participating in your old lifestyle, and that, my beloved, is the *overgrowth* that needs to be pruned from your life.

Jesus wants to do a mighty work in you and through you by means of the Holy Spirit! But if you're not letting Him cut the junk out of your life, then you're just not going to get that good healthy growth that you need to produce good, sweet fruit.

We're staring the new year in its face, and though I'm not big on new year's resolutions, maybe you need to make some changes in your lifestyle in order to let God receive some glory from your life story. I would like to challenge you, as I have done in my own life, to evaluate yourself. Give yourself a real honest assessment as to what you need to let the Vinedresser prune. He prunes whom He loves just as He chastens. If He didn't love you, then He would cut you off and throw you into the fire and be done with you, but that's not the God we were saved by! A God who let His beloved Son bear the sin of the world will *not* give up on you that easy.

As iron sharpens iron,
Just pray about it.

The Weight of Words

This comes from a very fresh conflict at work with a particular individual. I won't get into details since I feel they are irrelevant. But as I was dealing with the aftermath of my actions within myself and talking with a brother, I started receiving some scripture and conviction from, no doubt, the Holy Spirit, so I started trying to find the passages. I cheat when it comes to that (won't lie) and use Google to find the scripture references.

Through my search, the question circled through my mind: "Why don't you use your words to honor God even when you get angry or at least keep your mouth shut?" Jesus became angry but still was righteous in His actions when He tore up the money changers in the temple courtyard. But when I get angry, I'm not so righteous in my actions. But why? Why can't I hold my temper and not lose my head? We are supposed to reflect Jesus's righteousness all the time, right? Why is what we say in heated conflict so important? It goes much deeper than the simple *law* that we can't take back the words that are spoken, much deeper! Matthew 12:36–37 states, "But I say to you that for every idle word men may speak, they will give account of it in the day of judgment. For by your words you will be justified, and by your words you will be condemned." Amen or oh, me? I have much to give account for myself. Why do you think there's such a strict warning on speaking idle words? It's because of the power that is in our words. Matthew 18:18–19 states, "Assuredly, I say to you, whatever you bind on earth will be bound in heaven, and whatever you loose on earth will be loosed in heaven. Again I say to you that if two of you agree on earth concerning anything that they ask, it will be done for them by My Father in heaven."

Okay, well, we can't physically bind anything in heaven with our hands; but I will tell you that when we start to speak evil, or negatively, we bind the ministering spirits from working on our behalf. This covers an array of issues, so I want to focus on the opening thought. When, in our anger, we lash out and speak in such a way that is *not* righteous, we must be very careful. We can bind God's angels by helping the situation. We can bind blessings! And when we bind the heavenly hosts, we can also loosen curses and ill-content.

This concept may not be a very favorable topic for some, but there's no arguing with the red letters of Jesus. In my personal conflict, I personally feel that I had every right to get angry. I did *not*, however, have any right to act the way I did and throw an Irish fit. May each of us seek to learn how to throw a Jesus fit instead of a fit of the flesh. Please study these principles and read the scriptures before and after those which I listed. This topic will provoke a lot of thought on the matter.

As iron sharpens iron,
Just pray about it.

The Work Is Worth It

Do people outside of church know that you're a Christian? This is something that I've struggled with as I'm sure you have too (to some degree at least). There are a few different sides to this issue too. Let's say you've been working the same job around the same people, and you have been living the *common lifestyle*, and then you were saved. It's a strange situation trying to change your ways in front of the people who have known you to be as corrupt as them for all this time, right? That's a lot of peer pressure on someone. And to consider what I've learned about people, they haven't really grown up much since middle school when they thought it was cool to make fun of someone and bully them.

You'd figure that adults would be better, but they aren't. So there's that situation where other people give you a hard time about the positive changes in your life. Maybe because they're intimidated or simply just playing into Satan's service to keep you from doing right and making the changes. There are going to be people whom you're going to have to get away from. It's just one of those things.

When Jesus called the disciples into ministry, He told them to drop what they were doing, take no provisions with them, and follow Him. He didn't even give them time to tell their family where they were going or what they were doing. He said, "Follow Me"! So, you're going to have to accept that once you become a Christian, you will have to prune the vines. You will see relationships severed. It's only necessary for your spiritual growth.

And another side of it, you don't want to be an oddball. You want to fit in and have friends or keep the ones you had before, and after all, the people that you spend time around aren't bad people; they just don't see eye to eye with your spiritual beliefs. So just as long as you don't act *all churchy* around them, all is well.

Personally, I can't live like that. I am who I am. I can't keep myself straight, let alone two or three of me. So I am whom you see. Still, though, this involves peer pressure just the same as the first illustration. Well, Jesus said that if we deny Him in front of others, then He will deny us in front of His Father (Matthew 10:33 states, "But whoever denies Me before men, him I will also deny before My Father who is in heaven.) So there's that.

This one has worked on me for a while. So you find yourself backslidden, and you are not at your highest spiritual peak, and you naturally don't show clear evidence that you are a Christian though that is not your intent. When you do try to make changes, you're going to find that the world is not going to let you just easily slide by like all is well. The enemy roams about seeking whom he may devour, so when you try and do the right thing, you will run into opposition. It's in these times when you'll find out whom you can count on. Though there are good people in this world still, let the Spirit guide you to discern whom you can and can't trust. Don't expose your struggles and weaknesses to just anyone because once you're exposed, it's like blood to a shark. They will attack you.

The fact is, we aren't perfect. We are all going to fall short of the glory of God. A powerful tool to help you through day-to-day struggles is an accountability partner or prayer partner, someone whom you can really count on with the same like-mindedness and the same heart as you. That person will be there to hear you, give you advice, and pray for you when you need it and, in turn, will be able to count on you for the same support. We all need that support. I think that may be one of the main reasons why so many Christians live a defeated life today. It's because they don't have the support from their brothers/sisters in Christ. We must look after one another in this journey, and we must be willing to hold the line in battle.

Nehemiah was a prophet whom God put in a special place at a special time. The time was the fifth-century BC. The situation was one of distress. This is the post-exile that we learn about in the book of Daniel. Ezra was charged by God to build the Temple just before this. God called Nehemiah to build the wall around the city. So let's pick up in Nehemiah 2:17–20:

> Then I said to them, "You see the distress that we are in, how Jerusalem lies waste, and its gates are burned with fire. Come and let us build the wall of Jerusalem, that we may no longer be a reproach." And I told them of the hand of my God which had been good upon me, and also of the king's words that he had spoken to me. So they said "Let us rise up and build." Then they set their hands to this good work. But when Sanballat the Horonite, Tobiah the Ammonite official, and Geshem the Arab heard of it, they laughed at us and despised us and said, "What is this thing that you are doing? Will you rebel against the king?" So I answered them, and said to them, "The God of heaven Himself will prosper us; therefore we His servants will arise and build, but you have no heritage, or right or memorial in Jerusalem."

As it took the whole remnant to build the wall due to the opposition, it, too, shall take us working together, building one another up in faith and truth to survive the future that lies before us. Let's set our hands to this good work together so that God will prosper us.

> As iron sharpens iron,
> Just pray about it.

Tomorrow Isn't Promised

We all know that we aren't promised tomorrow. But are you ready? Are you really ready? Are you sure? If not, then what? What about the ones who think they are ready but don't know the truth?

I just started thinking about the people who have bought the lies and all the people who think that it's all about them, and the story of Lazarus and the rich man came to mind. Luke 16:19–31 states:

> There was a certain rich man who was clothed in purple and fine linen and fared sumptuously every day. But there was a certain beggar named Lazarus, full of sores, who was laid at his gate, desiring to be fed with the crumbs which fell from the rich man's table. Moreover, the dogs came and licked his sores. So it was that the beggar died and was carried by the angels to Abraham's bosom. The rich man also died and was buried. And being in torments in Hades, he lifted up his eyes and saw Abraham afar off, and Lazarus in his bosom. Then he cried and said, "Father Abraham, have mercy on me, and send Lazarus that he may dip the tip of his finger in water and cool my tongue; for I am tormented in this flame." But Abraham said, "Son, remember that in your lifetime you received your good things, and likewise

Lazarus evil things; but now he is comforted and you are tormented. And besides all this, between us and you there is a great gulf fixed, so that those who want to pass from here to you cannot, nor can those from there pass to us." Then he said, "I beg you therefore, father, that you would send him to my father's house, for I have five brothers that he may testify to them, lest they also come to this place of torment." Abraham said to him, "They have Moses and the prophets; let them hear them." And he said, "No, father Abraham; but if one goes to them from the dead, they will repent." But he said to him, "If they do not hear Moses and the prophets, neither will they be persuaded though one rise from the dead."

Let's say the rich man will signify all the people who have stepped over the truth of salvation in order to obtain their personal happiness in this life. And while we're at it, we can add to this category the people who believe that there are other ways to get to heaven instead of only through Jesus Christ. And Lazarus will stand in place of all the Christians who, in due time, will receive their reward and deliverance from the suffering of this world which lies in heaven.

Now the unbeliever has gone through life thinking that it's all about them or has diluted the truth and has taken the Living Word out of context in order to make it fit their lives so they don't have to change. One day, they are going to wake up in eternal agony that will be so great there will be screams of torment and gnashing of the teeth. Don't find yourself in that late hour like the rich man, looking up to heaven where you see people you knew who have lived their lives as a true and faithful witness and tried to share the truth with you and has tried to get you to wake up spending countless hours praying that you would see the light, walking around in splendor with the Great Comforter as you wish that just one of them would look down and feel sorry for you enough that they would come down and give you just a tiny bit of comfort because, at that point, you have made your bed. And I tell you, my beloved, you will lie in the bed you have made. But instead, make sure you are the one who is poor in spirit such as this beggar Lazarus. (Don't lose this key point about being poor in spirit. That doesn't mean destitute as the Hebrew word *ebyown*. But rather, the Greek word as it was used here is *peno*, which means to toil (or work hard to obtain) for daily sustenance.)

Matthew 5:3 states, "Blessed *are* the poor in spirit, for theirs is the kingdom of heaven."

I want to get back to the rich man because he found himself floating down a swollen creek without a paddle or plan. He thought he had it all and on earth, I guess he did. So many people have it all but lack the one and only important thing that anyone can obtain—a personal relationship with Jesus Christ. Whosoever passes through this life into the next without confessing their sins to God and believing that Jesus was in fact crucified on the cross, died, and three days later arose from the grave conquering death will find themselves sitting beside the rich man wailing and gnashing teeth wishing someone would go and tell their loved ones the truth. Don't let that be you.

Jesus went down to the pits of hell and conquered death, paying our sin debt with His life so we wouldn't have to. He was where the rich man is, but glory be to God that He is powerful enough and loving enough to give us the opportunity to say, "Death is swallowed up in victory. O Death, where is your sting? O Hell, where is your victory?" (1 Corinthians 15:54–55).

As iron sharpens iron,
Just pray about it.

We Are More than Conquerors

Why do we have problems with besetting sins? I wonder this sometimes how if we are more than conquerors through Jesus Christ, and according to Paul, we are no longer slaves to sin, then why do we continue to fall into that? Why do we walk around with our guard down? Is it more complicated? Maybe it's more simplified than anything, and we're simply missing it altogether. Could we just simply be too busy to take the proper steps to obtain the strength and fortification we need to withstand the temptations of the flesh? I'm sure that you all have heard this teaching before: "We are all born with a God-sized void in our heart." And that being the case, then we struggle day by day trying to fill it with the earthly garbage, which leads us to fall into temptation.

You think that's why Jesus told us to take up our cross daily and follow Him? If we do that first thing in the morning, it would be just like suiting up for battle. Think premeditated battle where soldiers had time to put on their armor, sharpen their swords, warm up a bit to get ready, go over a game plan even, and study their enemy's tactics so they can be more prepared. Hmm! Let's see! Ephesians 6:10–17 states:

> Finally, my brethren, be strong in the Lord and in the power of His might. Put on the whole armor of God, that you may be able to stand against the wiles of the devil. For we do not wrestle against flesh and blood, but against principalities, against powers, against the rulers

of the darkness of this age, against spiritual hosts of wickedness in the heavenly places. Therefore take up the whole armor of God, that you may be able to withstand in the evil day, and having done all, to stand. Stand therefore, having girded your waist with truth, having put on the breastplate of righteousness, and having shod your feet with the preparation of the gospel of peace; above all, taking the shield of faith with which you will be able to quench the fiery darts of the wicked one. And take the helmet of salvation, and the sword of the Spirit, which is the word of God.

Just think of how effective we could be if we lived our lives with this feeling fresh, not just an afterthought. We can't continue to live defeated lives because Jesus didn't die in vain! I would love to be a part of such a humble group of people who would dare to be emboldened by the Holy Spirit to stand in the gap! Just as the men of renown in the valley of the dry bones, the great army of the Lord, revived and standing ready! Who will stand beside me as my brother and sister in Christ to hold me accountable as we do so with each other? Let this be more than just a pep talk to get your feelers tingling! Let this be the start of a revival that will sweep across our land. Some forest fires start with a simple spark; others start by lighting. Hey, whatever it takes, whatever works!

As iron sharpens iron,
Just pray about it.

What Can You Live Without?

How many people do you know, if asked, would say that they don't want to go to heaven? There are going to be people who more frequently say they don't need heaven due to the moral decay of civilization, but honestly, this is the Bible belt, right? If you get down to it, many people would say no simply because at the first thought of heaven, it automatically makes them feel unworthy because of their sin. For the most part, people know and understand that they are dirty ole wretched people who can't make it to heaven on their own. And they're right. But what they don't realize is how easy it is to be saved and actually get to heaven! Take a walk down the Roman Road with me.

Romans 3:23 states:

> For all have sinned and fall short of the glory of God.

Romans 6:23 states:

> For the wages of sin is death but the gift of God is eternal life.

Romans 10:9–10 states:

> That if you confess with your mouth the Lord Jesus and believe in your heart that God has raised Him from the dead, you will be saved. For

> with the heart one believes unto righteousness, and with the mouth confession is made unto salvation.

This is known in evangelism studies as the Roman Road to salvation. It's straightforward and to the point and tells you just what you have to do to become saved. It's at this point that the Holy Spirit will take up residence in your heart and start to do a mighty work in you that nobody on this earth can do. He will convict you of your wrong. He will guide you to do right. He will even guide your steps on the path you should go.

Of course, it's ultimately up to us to follow the path He sends us down. I'm here to tell you, friend, that the path is not an easy one. Anyone who tells you that the path to righteousness is easy is lying to you for whatever reason so you will give up, or they simply don't know that they themselves are lost. Being a Christian is hard when you live in a world that is governed by a serpent. Look here at what Jesus has to say about the pathway to heaven. Matthew 7:13–14 states:

> Enter by the narrow gate; for wide is the gate and broad is the way that leads to destruction, and there are many who go in by it. Because narrow is the gate and difficult is the way which leads to life, and there are few who find it.

Are we really living our Christian lives seeking the narrow gate? What does that even mean? It means what He says in the same chapter, verse 21 (Matthew 7:21), "Not everyone who says to Me, 'Lord, Lord,' shall enter the kingdom of heaven, but he who does the will of My Father in heaven." The passage that actually led me to write this is Matthew 5:29–30:

> If your right eye causes you to sin, pluck it out and cast it from you; for it is more profitable that one of your members perish, than for your

whole body to be cast into hell. And if your right
hand causes you to sin, cut it off and cast it from
you; for it is more profitable for you that one of
your members perish, than for your whole body
to be cast into hell.

Don't maim yourself and blame me for it. I honestly feel there
are more simplified ways to minimize temptation than actually physically plucking out your eye or cutting off your hand. At least there
are less-destructive starting points. Just this evening, I deleted (again)
my social media accounts, both Facebook and Instagram, because
they were posing a severe hindrance to my devotion time to God. I've
deleted the apps off my phone a few different times, but this time, I
deleted the accounts.

They didn't just pose a distraction, but it's so easy to be tempted
and enticed to follow that broad path that leads to destruction. If you
don't have a problem in that area, then by all means continue. There's
a lot of good that can come from properly utilizing social media plat-
forms! I wasn't using them for any good. Let's say that I plucked out
one of my eyes that was causing me to sin.

Whatever it may be, I'd like to encourage you to search your
heart, listen to the Holy Spirit as He tells you what is hindering you
from getting close to the Father, and ask for divine help to cut that
off. It may be difficult to let it go possibly, then again maybe not.
But regardless, it will be worth it. Bear in mind that I'm not telling
you what it is that is coming between you and God. It's none of my
business! But you know what it is.

As iron sharpens iron,
Just pray about it.

Wolves in Sheep's Clothing

Do you wonder why it seems that so many church assemblies have so many problems? It's like sometimes they get torn apart from within. And sometimes, it's over the simplest things like the color paint in this hallway or that room or the color of the carpet, or maybe the fact that those shrubs were planted by this person's momma and shouldn't be taken up; yet they don't even take care of them, to begin with. No, I personally haven't had any firsthand experiences with any of this that I can recall. But I've heard a story or two about it. What about doctrinal issues? This I have had a small taste of, but it wasn't bad enough to break up the fellowship, not when I was at an assembly anyway.

No matter what problems an assembly faces, it should never be enough to break it up! Jesus said that where two or three gather in His name, there He will be also. That means *we* are the church if, in fact, we gather in His name! Not that building. That is just a gathering or assembly area. So if we are the church, why do we let such things happen?

I understand that some people have compatibility issues with others, and there are some personalities that clash. I'm not naïve enough to not understand that. I'm certain that I get on some people's nerves. Get in line, sometimes I get on my own nerves! But seriously, beloved, can we not simply stand on the fact that we have a commonality in and through Christ Jesus who spared not His own life so as to establish His church by and through us? So where does that leave us then?

Just for a moment, let's take out all the denominational differences. There are forty-one thousand Christian denominations across the globe according to a random Google search I just did. Not all those denominations agree on everything, yet we all believe and affirm that Jesus was born to a virgin, lived in the flesh for thirty-some years, died on the cross, defeated death and hell, paid our sin debt with His blood, and then ascended into heaven to return one day that only the Father knows when to receive to Himself His bridegroom. And to call yourself a Christian fellowship, that is the basic requisites as well as having to confess that we are broken sinners in need of a Savior due to our own sin.

I've been to Mexico on a couple of different trips where I experienced worship like no other time before. And it leads me to wonder how people who know nothing about the *legalistic* aspect of church can be filled with the Holy Spirit, yet with all the *churches* here in the United States, there are so many issues. What are we doing? Where are we failing? Are we so legalized in our assemblies today that we miss what we're even here for?

In Mark 7, Jesus warns about traditionalism and how getting lost in that had caused the people to lose sight of the real perspective. The Pharisees were the most religiously educated people of their time, and they were so legalized that they had forsaken what God had established in the original covenant. They rejected the prophecies that spoke of His first coming. And the worst part of that was the fact that He was right in front of their faces. Even the Pharisees were looking for Him to come and restore the Jewish kingdom, but they were so wrapped up in the image they had painted for themselves that they couldn't see the forest for the trees. They had developed their own way of things that they didn't want to admit or believe that He was whom He said He was. They had a certain authoritative role that they didn't want to lose. Matthew 7:15–20 states:

> Beware of false prophets who come to you in
> sheep's clothing, but inwardly they are ravenous
> wolves. You will know them by their fruits. Do
> men gather grapes from thornbushes or figs from

thistles? Even so, every good tree bears good fruit, but a bad tree bears bad fruit. A good tree cannot bear bad fruit, nor can a bad tree bear good fruit. Every tree that does not bear good fruit is cut down and thrown into the fire. Therefore by their fruits, you will know them.

From the day that Jesus's earthly ministry started, after He was baptized and was fasting, Satan was after Him. And that forked tongue serpent has done everything he can think of since to infiltrate the church. And in so many cases, many of the assembly's members have opened the door for him and his minions to come in. So how do we combat this issue? To start with, we must test the spirits.

In 1 John 4:1–3, it states:

> Beloved, do not believe every spirit, but test the spirits, whether they are of God; because many false prophets have gone out into the world. By this, you know the Spirit of God: Every spirit that confesses that Jesus Christ has come in the flesh is of God, and every spirit that does not confess that Jesus Christ has come in the flesh is not of God. And this is the spirit of the Antichrist, which you have heard was coming and is now already in the world.

With every issue that ever has been presented or is to be presented, God left us instructions in His Word on how to deal with them. Do we know the Word enough to be able to lean on what it says to handle such issues, or are we taking others' word on what to do? Do we test the spirits and reference the infallible Word of God on matters? Can we, for ourselves, discern matters with enough clarity to know when we've been handed a load of junk contrary to God's Word?

I personally feel that if I studied the Word more than I study other things, then I wouldn't doubt my discerning capabilities to handle trials and problems. And I personally believe that Jesus's church wouldn't have the problem of infiltration. First off, we would be able to catch the wolves at the door. And we would be able to lay aside our differences and find common ground and rest in our faith and belief that Jesus is who He is. Be vigilant for the ravenous wolves of this day who will sell half-truths and sow division among the assembly.

> As iron sharpens iron,
> Just pray about it.

Worship Him

In the Ten Commandments, we're told not to have any other gods before the one true living God. The second one says not to make nor take for ourselves a carved image to bow down to which means not to have an idol to worship. In the minds of so many, they think along the lines that they'll never do something like that. Mental imagery makes one think of worshiping things you'd think about the way Muslims throw down their prayer rug and face east and start praying in their way at certain times of the day.

Well, what would you say if I told you that anything you let take up your time is what you worship? You can take anything good and turn it into something sinful by putting it before God. For example, hunting is great! It's fun and relaxing; it adds meat to your freezer (and judging by the prices in the grocery store, I personally need the help). And while hunting, being in nature, you can use the time to get closer to God. You can also spend too much time wrapping yourself into it and lose sight of every good thing that is there to partake of. Fishing is the same way, as well as sports and work, and actually, you can put your family in front of God and lose sight of the most important truth: God has given you all things, and we should rejoice, be glad in it, and praise and worship God Almighty.

He needs the credit, He wants a relationship with us, and He deserves our fellowship. So why do we tend to put things in front of God? I personally feel that it stems from our selfish nature. Since the fall of man, we are all born into the law of sin, so we are born broken in nature. But bear in mind that God appointed it unto man *once* to die, then the Judgment. He doesn't want us to be condemned to death like the fallen angels. He didn't create hell for us; He created it for Satan and the fallen angels.

Take a look at this: My Bible has Isaiah 46 titled "the power of God and the powerlessness of idols." Isaiah 46:1–5 states:

> Bel bows down, Nebo stoops; their idols were on the beasts and on the cattle. Your carriages were heavily loaded, a burden to the weary beast. They stoop, they bow down together; they could not deliver the burden, but have themselves gone into captivity. "Listen to Me, O house of Jacob, and all the remnant of the house of Israel, who have been upheld by Me from birth, who have been carried from the womb: Even to your old age, I am He, and even to gray hairs I will carry you! I have made, and I will bear; even I will carry, and will deliver you. To whom will you liken Me, and make Me equal and compare Me, that we should be alike?"

Isn't it awesome to be created by a God that gives us promise after promise that all our needs will be taken care of, and He will carry us from the womb to our old age? Yes, He does say that He's a jealous God, but aren't we the least bit jealous of our spouses? Not dangerously jealous where we make the other miserable when they speak to someone else but jealous to the point that when we see another trying to get too close to them, we get defensive. We don't want someone else to come and get them distracted.

There are a lot of silver tongue devils in this world just as there are a bunch of wolves in sheep's clothing seeking whom they may devour. We don't want that for our spouses or children any more than God wants that for us. That's why He doesn't want us to put anything else in front of Him and why He's jealous. He wants the best for us, but we can't expect to shack up with the devil during the week and have God pay the rent. He yearns for us to spend time with Him. He desires for our fellowship, and He deserves our undivided worship—not a worship that is being shared with other gods that we put in front of Him but a worship that belongs to Him alone.

As iron sharpens iron,
Just pray about it.

You Are Chosen

No matter where you are in your life right now, God wants you to know that He has chosen you to fulfill a mission. No human being can fathom God's insight on their life unless He chooses to show them. You don't know what He has in store for you nor what He has called you to do! In 1 Corinthians 2:9, it states, "But as it is written: 'Eye has not seen, nor ear heard, nor have entered into the heart of man the things which God has prepared for those who love Him.'"

And I don't want you to look at this from the wrong point of view here, so just stay with me. Don't approach this in a negative mindset but rather with a positive mindset. There's so much *more* than what you can possibly expect. It's more than average. In fact, it's more than majestically beyond your wildest comprehension as to what He has called you for. I can only imagine that there's someone reading this who's in a rut, and you're probably thinking to yourself, *There's no way that God called a screw up like me into any service of His. This dude has me messed up with someone else.*

But I'm here to tell you, neighbor, you're wrong! God called you! You want to know how I know God called you into service for Him? Because He chose you to be born at the very moment you were born, conceived even. Yes, even at conception when your life actually started, He called you and set you apart for a special ministry for the exact circumstances you face day to day. Circumstances that only your life experiences have prepared you for. That's how awesome and mighty His plan is for you! Jeremiah 1:5 states, "Before I formed you in the womb I knew you; before you were born I sanctified you; I ordained you a prophet to the nations."

Just because these were the words of God to a prophet named Jeremiah in the sixth-century BC, do we discount them? Certainly not! Jesus said that we would be greater than the prophets of old if we just exercised the faith to activate the Holy Spirit within us. Okay, so this message has found you in a bad spot in your life. So! Guess what? It's just one more feather in your hat, friend! One more notch in your belt. One more experience that you can relate to when you're given that opportunity to be a witness for Him to a lost and dying world!

You think this is just a pep talk? Well, it's not. Even if this message hasn't found you in a bad spot, but you're simply dormant or inactive, it's all the same. All this time by one means or another, He has been preparing you for that glorious day when you rise up out of that valley of dry bones, and you stand in the gap for your friend, your coworker, or your family member who is on the highway to hell; and you stand at the ready to take the fight to Satan's doorstep.

Ezekiel 37:1–14 states:

> The hand of the Lord came upon me and brought me out in the Spirit of the Lord and set me down in the midst of the valley; and it was full of bones. Then He caused me to pass by them all around, and behold, there were very many in the open valley; and indeed they were very dry. And He said to me, "Son of man, can these bones live?" So I answered, "O Lord God, You know." Again He said to me, "Prophesy to these bones, and say to them, 'O dry bones, hear the word of the Lord! Thus says the Lord God to these bones: "Surely I will cause breath to enter into you, and you shall live. I will put sinews on you and bring flesh upon you, cover you with skin and put breath in you; and you shall live. Then you shall know that I am the Lord." So I prophesied as I was commanded; and as I prophesied, there was

a noise, and suddenly a rattling; and the bones came together, bone to bone. Indeed, as I looked, the sinews and the flesh came upon them, and the skin covered them over; but there was no breath in them. Also He said to me, "Prophesy to the breath, prophesy, son of man, and say to the [a]breath, 'Thus says the Lord God: "Come from the four winds, O breath, and breathe on these slain, that they may live." So I prophesied as He commanded me, and [b]breath came into them, and they lived, and stood upon their feet, an exceedingly great army. Then He said to me, "Son of man, these bones are the whole house of Israel. They indeed say, 'Our bones are dry, our hope is lost, and we ourselves are cut off!' Therefore prophesy and say to them, 'Thus says the Lord God: "Behold, O My people, I will open your graves and cause you to come up from your graves and bring you into the land of Israel. Then you shall know that I am the Lord, when I have opened your graves, O My people, and brought you up from your graves. I will put My Spirit in you, and you shall live, and I will place you in your own land. Then you shall know that I, the Lord, have spoken it and performed it," says the Lord.

If you were truly born again, then that means the Holy Spirit has resided in your heart when you confessed your sins to God and asked Jesus Christ to be a part of your life and to be your Lord and Savior. Remember, after Jesus was resurrected from the grave, He told His followers that He must go in order to make room for the Great Counselor to work on our behalf! This is what Jesus was talking about! He was teaching them one last thing. That it will only be through them exercising their faith that they will be able to do great and mighty work!

No matter where you are right now or where you've been, let today be your day when you breathe in the breath of the four winds that come from the Lord God Almighty! Let this day be the day that is declared to be when flesh and sinew cover the dry bones and the great army of the one true God stands united in faith! Let today be the day that you take up the whole armor of God so that you may be able to withstand all the fiery darts of the enemy.

As iron sharpens iron,
Just pray about it.

About the Author

Everything that is written from the author's hand comes from God as He has given him the perception of His Word. Ryan Brown writes as a layman. Though he does have some education, he has no degrees to show for it. He's actually a lineman by trade, so he has a slightly different take on things than others. He believes that a message should be practical so anyone can understand it, yet in-depth so the point should not be missed. All the scriptures come from the New King James Version Bible, and he does not change the scriptures that he uses. The author encourages you to open your Bibles and test the spirits with every teaching that is presented to you, especially his! We live in troubling times and false prophets, and Antichrists are rising up all over, and it's imperative that you stay in the Word and hold every teacher and every author accountable by weighing every word written with Truth. Ryan's hope is for every reader to be challenged by what is written and encouraged to stay in the Word. Proverbs 27:17 states, "As iron sharpens iron, so a man sharpens the countenance of his friend."

www.ingramcontent.com/pod-product-compliance
Lightning Source LLC
Chambersburg PA
CBHW061356160726
47995CB00001B/347